Acting Edition

HANG TIME

by Zora Howard

‖SAMUEL FRENCH‖

Copyright © 2025 by Zora Howard
All Rights Reserved

HANG TIME is fully protected under the copyright laws of the United States of America, the British Commonwealth, including Canada, and all member countries of the Berne Convention for the Protection of Literary and Artistic Works, the Universal Copyright Convention, and/or the World Trade Organization conforming to the Agreement on Trade Related Aspects of Intellectual Property Rights. All rights, including professional and amateur stage productions, recitation, lecturing, public reading, motion picture, radio broadcasting, television, online/digital production, and the rights of translation into foreign languages are strictly reserved.

ISBN 978-0-573-71104-6

www.concordtheatricals.com
www.concordtheatricals.co.uk

FOR PRODUCTION INQUIRIES

UNITED STATES AND CANADA
info@concordtheatricals.com
1-866-979-0447

UNITED KINGDOM AND EUROPE
licensing@concordtheatricals.co.uk
020-7054-7298

Each title is subject to availability from Concord Theatricals Corp., depending upon country of performance. Please be aware that *HANG TIME* may not be licensed by Concord Theatricals Corp. in your territory. Professional and amateur producers should contact the nearest Concord Theatricals Corp. office or licensing partner to verify availability.

CAUTION: Professional and amateur producers are hereby warned that *HANG TIME* is subject to a licensing fee. The purchase, renting, lending or use of this book does not constitute a license to perform this title(s), which license must be obtained from Concord Theatricals Corp. prior to any performance. Performance of this title(s) without a license is a violation of federal law and may subject the producer and/or presenter of such performances to civil penalties. Both amateurs and professionals considering a production are strongly advised to apply to the appropriate agent before starting rehearsals, advertising, or booking a theatre. A licensing fee must be paid whether the title(s) is presented for charity or gain and whether or not admission is charged. Professional/Stock licensing fees are quoted upon application to Concord Theatricals Corp.

This work is published by Samuel French, an imprint of Concord Theatricals Corp.

No one shall make any changes in this title(s) for the purpose of production. No part of this book may be reproduced, stored in a retrieval system, scanned, uploaded, or transmitted in any form, by any means, now known or yet to be invented, including mechanical, electronic, digital, photocopying, recording, videotaping, or otherwise, without the prior written permission of the publisher. No one shall share this title(s), or any part of this title(s), through any social media or file hosting websites.

For all inquiries regarding motion picture, television, online/digital and other media rights, please contact Concord Theatricals Corp.

MUSIC AND THIRD-PARTY MATERIALS USE NOTE

Licensees are solely responsible for obtaining formal written permission from copyright owners to use copyrighted music and/or other copyrighted third-party materials (e.g. artworks, logos) in the performance of this play and are strongly cautioned to do so. If no such permission is obtained by the licensee, then the licensee must use only original music and materials that the licensee owns and controls. Licensees are solely responsible and liable for clearances of all third-party copyrighted materials, including without limitation music, and shall indemnify the copyright owners of the play(s) and their licensing agent, Concord Theatricals Corp., against any costs, expenses, losses and liabilities arising from the use of such copyrighted third-party materials by licensees. For music, please contact the appropriate music licensing authority in your territory for the rights to any incidental music.

IMPORTANT BILLING AND CREDIT REQUIREMENTS

If you have obtained performance rights to this title, please refer to your licensing agreement for important billing and credit requirements.

HANG TIME received its world premiere at The Flea (Niegel Smith, Executive Artistic Director; Martin Meccouri, Director of Producing) in New York City on March 17, 2023. The production was directed by Zora Howard, with scenic design by Neal Wilkinson, costume design by Dominique Fawn Hill, lighting design by Reza Behjat, sound design by Megan Culley, and movement direction by Charlie Oates. The production stage manager was Beatrice Pérez-Arche. The cast was as follows:

BIRD . . . . Dion Graham
SLIM . . . . Akron Watson
BLOOD . . . . Cecil Blutcher

A workshop production of *HANG TIME*, directed by Zora Howard, was presented as a part of the 2021 Ojai Playwrights Conference New Work Festival (Robert Egan, Artistic Director/Producer).

HANG TIME was additionally developed at Seattle Rep and The Lark.

CHARACTERS

BIRD – (M), Black, sixties. Has seen some things. Knows to keep his head down.

SLIM – (M), Black, forties. The pontificatin' type. Quick to tell you the way of the world.

BLOOD – (M), Black, twenties. Just coming into himself.

SETTING

Underneath an old, wide tree.

TIME

Anytime. All the time.

NOTES ON STYLE

A speech usually follows the one immediately before it except when:

a) one character starts speaking before the other has finished, and the point of interruption is marked "/".

b) there are multiple interruptions, which will be marked sequentially by "/", "//", "///", etc.

A **Pivot** marks a kind of resetting. It is four times as long whatever you think a beat is. Or even longer. Listen for it.

In general, the play takes its time. It should run an hour long.

AUTHOR'S NOTE

In the summer of 2020, two Black men were found hanging in Southern California within weeks of one another. Robert Fuller and Malcolm Harsch. Buried under countless "breaking news" stories, there was scant coverage about their deaths. I could not stop thinking of the two men, the lives they might have lived. Moreover, I could not figure out how to archive these deeply personal and public violences in my own consciousness and body. I needed somewhere to reckon with that question. *HANG TIME* was born out of that need.

> *Three men chew the fat under an old wide tree.*

HANG TIME is a "sitting and talking" play. But instead of sitting and talking, the three Black men at the play's center are hanging as if from a tree. Yet there is no tree in the play's design, nor any other element that delineates time or place. The usual trappings of the theater are intentionally absent. The standalone set piece – a technical apparatus that suspends the actors' bodies in space – is the only reference the audience will have to contextualize the violence in the play's central image.

And, even still, with all of its implied brutality, *HANG TIME* invites the viewer to envisage the Black body triumphant over the legacy of violence that it holds. Within these pages, Bird, Slim and Blood are alive. They talk shit, they make plans, they remember. They, like the rest of us, cannot play their end.

For sixty minutes in the dark, they do not hang "3,000 miles away," or in the "Jim Crow South." They hang here here here, now now now.

– Zora Howard

For Robert Leroy Butler the First, Second and Third.

Also for Claude, Alexandre and Zachary. My menfolk.

(Darkness. Cicadas.)

SLIM. Mmm, mmm, mmm.

Now ain't that a sight for sore eyes.

BIRD. What?

SLIM. Over there.

BIRD. Over where?

SLIM. Is you blind, nigga? Look.

Look look look. Quick.

BLOOD. Where?

BIRD. Oh. I see.

SLIM. Oooweeee, sure *is* somethin' to see, ain't it.

BLOOD. Oh yeah, I see now.

BIRD. That's alright right there.

SLIM. More than alright right there.

Can't even look away if I wanted to.

BIRD. Can't even.

*(Lights slowly fill the space. Three **MEN** hanging from an old wide tree. They shoot the shit.)*

SLIM. She comin' round the corner.

BIRD. Yeah?

SLIM. Ooooo, she comin' round the corner when she come!

BIRD. When she come.

SLIM. I can already tell.

BLOOD. Tell what?

SLIM. Too much ripple in them hips and too much tittle in them tits for there not to be some brass...in that ass.

BLOOD. Ha!

BIRD. *(Affirming.)* Is a lotta tittle.

BLOOD. Didn't know you were a poet, Slim.

SLIM. Oh, Imma poet.

Imma poet and a lotta thangs, youngblood.

Poet and a lotta thangs.

BIRD. She turning now.

SLIM. O, here we go here we go here we go

(To **BLOOD.***)* Pay attention.

(The **MEN** *follow with their eyes.)*

BLOOD. Damn.

SLIM. *(Vindicated.)* Am I lyin' or am I dyin'?

BIRD. Damn.

SLIM. I said am I lyin' or am I dyin'?!

BIRD. Well, you ain't lyin'.

SLIM. GOT damn.

BLOOD. Yeah, that's somethin' there.

BIRD. Lordy lord lord.

SLIM. Ass clap like that make you wanna clap back.

Standin' ovation kind of ass right there.

BLOOD. Ha!

SLIM. Make you wanna call somebody.

BIRD. Be somebody.

SLIM. Do right by ya mama.

BIRD. Do right by ya God.

SLIM. Shid, pay your bills on time.

BIRD. Just make the space around it look different.

SLIM. Make the sun a little brighter.

BIRD. Shade a little cooler.

SLIM. Amen and amen!

Yeah, that's a Sunday kinda ass right there.

BLOOD. Sunday kinda ass?

SLIM. Make every day feel like Sunday kinda ass right there.

> *(The **MEN** continue looking after the woman until she passes out of sight.)*
>
> *(Pause.)*

BIRD. ...Is it Sunday?

SLIM. Think so.

BLOOD. Yeah, think so.

SLIM. Everything closed so...

BLOOD. Must be.

BIRD. Yeah, must be.

> *(Beat.)*

SLIM. Knew me a woman like that once.

BLOOD. Yeah?

SLIM. Sure did.

(Remembering.) Boy, I tell you / –

(**BIRD** *snorts.*)

SLIM. *(Off* **BIRD.***)* What?

BIRD. Blood, you got time?

BLOOD. Yeah, I got time.

BIRD. Good. Cause Slim 'bout to talk you near to death.

SLIM. Shut up, Bird.

BLOOD. I got time.

SLIM. Nah. I don't feel like talkin' no more.

BIRD. Oh, now you don't feel like talkin'?

SLIM. Nope.

BIRD. Nigga, you always feel like talkin'.

SLIM. Not when no one appreciates what I'm sayin'.

BLOOD. We appreciate it, Slim.

BIRD. Speak for yourself.

SLIM. No need wastin' my breath.

BIRD. Fine. Don't say shit then.

SLIM. I won't say shit then.

BIRD. Mmhmm.

(Pause.)

SLIM. *(Can't help himself.)* ...She really was somethin', though.

(**BIRD** *snorts.*)

Brick house of a woman.

Dark and tender.

Just a juicy / ol' thang –

BIRD. We talkin' 'bout broads or we talkin' 'bout chicken?

SLIM. Sharp like a blade and quick like a pistol.

Man, she was bad!

BLOOD. Sound like it.

SLIM. You ever made love to a woman make you forget yourself?

Man, listen. First time she laid it on me, changed my whole life.

Quit my job. Changed my religion. Learned Creole behind that woman.

You think I'm playing? I'm tellin' you. There's no place too far. No valley high or mountain low. You will go to the ends of the Earth for a woman do you like that.

Drive you mad. That loving thing? Drive you out your mind mad.

BLOOD. Well, what happened to her?

SLIM. Came home one night and found her laid up with some nigga that wasn't me.

BLOOD. Damn.

SLIM. Yeah, I was cut up about it.

BLOOD. Damn.

SLIM. Wasn't cut through like that nigga was though. Ha!

BLOOD. Cut through?

SLIM. Mmhmm. Sliced that nigga straight through. Nose to navel.

*(**BLOOD** looks at **SLIM**.)*

BLOOD. ...You killed him?

*(**SLIM** looks at **BLOOD**.)*

SLIM. Do I look like a killer to you?

>   (**BIRD** *grunts.*)

BLOOD. That's crazy.

SLIM. Make you crazy, loving somebody.

Make you do what you won't do.

BLOOD. Hmm.

>   (*Pause.*)

SLIM. (*To* **BLOOD**.) You got you somebody?

BLOOD. Me?

BIRD. He ain't askin' me.

BLOOD. Oh.

...

Yeah, something like it.

SLIM. Something like it?

BLOOD. Yeah…

SLIM. I'm talkin' 'bout somebody make your groin ache and heart palpitate at the same damn time. I ain't talkin' 'bout no "something like it."

BLOOD. Well, I don't know then.

SLIM. You love her?

BLOOD. You sure ask a lot of questions.

SLIM. Nah, ain't askin' no questions.

We just shootin' the breeze, Blood.

Chewin' the fat. Ain't no thang.

>   (*Pause.*)

Come on, you either love the broad or you don't.

(**BLOOD** *sucks his teeth.*)

Oh, I see. I see what it is. I see what it is, playa.

...

You two-timing that broad, ain't you?

BLOOD. Man, what?

SLIM. Three-timing?

BLOOD. I ain't two-timing nothing.

SLIM. *(Re:* **BLOOD.***)* Look at him getting all red in the face. Look at him, Bird. Ha!

BLOOD. Man, get out of here.

SLIM. Aww, why you getting all flustered, Youngblood? Shid, ain't me you laid up with.

BLOOD. I don't like niggas interrogating me.

SLIM. Who's interrogating?

Bird, you interrogating?

BIRD. Leave the boy alone.

SLIM. Awww, we just talking man to man to man is all.

That's it. Ain't mean no harm.

(Pause; relenting.)

But that's alright.

A Pivot.

BLOOD. Pretty day.

Hot.

(Pause.)

BIRD. Good weather for growing greens.

...

BIRD. Cabbage

...

Hotter than usual for the season, though.

BLOOD. Yeah?

BIRD. Mmmhmm.

BLOOD. I can't call it.

Guess it's hard to tell this close to the water.

BIRD. Mmmhmm.

BLOOD. Nice either way.

BIRD. Mmmhmm.

BLOOD. Real nice.

> *(Pause.)*

Ever been down there?

BIRD. Down where?

BLOOD. The water.

BIRD. Nope.

BLOOD. Slim?

SLIM. Nah, ain't never been.

BIRD. All these years living by it, never been in it.

BLOOD. Oh...

> *(Pause.)*

Ever wonder where it let out?

BIRD. Never seemed like much to see down there.

SLIM. Dock...fishermen.

BLOOD. But where it goes?

BIRD. S'pose it go to some ocean.

BLOOD. And after that?

BIRD. After that?

SLIM. After that?

BIRD. No idea.

> *(Pause.)*

SLIM. Pay day tomorrow.

BIRD. Hmm.

BLOOD. Already?

SLIM. That's right.

BIRD. Can't keep up.

SLIM. With your money?

Dangerous way.

BIRD. I don't borrow and I don't lend.

That's no danger at all.

SLIM. Well, since you so lackadaisical about your dollars...

let me hold a lil' somethin'.

BIRD. Nigga, did you hear what I just said?

SLIM. Awww, c'mon, Bird. Just lil' somethin'.

...Pay you interest.

BIRD. No.

SLIM. Ten percent. Can't beat that with a crooked stick.

BIRD. No.

SLIM. Alright seven. But I'm not going no higher.

BIRD. Nigga, you can go high as Kilimanjaro all I care.

SLIM. You a hateful nigga, you know that?

(**BIRD** *grunts.*)

SLIM. Just bitter.

BIRD. Guess I am.

SLIM. ...Please?

(**BIRD** *doesn't budge.*)

Forget you then.

(*Changing his approach.*) ...Blo/od...?

BLOOD. Can't even help you, Slim.

SLIM. Man, forget y'all both.

Don't need your help.

...Help myself.

BIRD. I pray to see the day.

SLIM. Yeah, whatever.

Thought that great big book of yours say give and ye shall receive.

BIRD. Book also say man who don't work, don't eat.

SLIM. I work. I work all the time.

BIRD. Where you / work?

SLIM. Don't ask me where I work, nigga.

...

You don't work.

BIRD. No, sir, but I have *worked*.

SLIM. Yeah, well, I don't do just any ol' kinda work, Bird.

BIRD. No, nigga, you don't do *any* work. Don't matter the kind.

SLIM. We not the same.

BIRD. Slim, what's them two things you got dangling below your wrists?

SLIM. Nigga, what?

BIRD. Them two things you got dangling below your wrists.

BLOOD. I think he talkin' 'bout your hands.

(**SLIM** *looks down.*)

SLIM. Man, whatever.

BIRD. You should try 'em out and see what happens. Might surprise you.

SLIM. You don't know what I do, nigga. And you don't know what I've done.

Talk about what you know about.

BIRD. Alright, Slim.

SLIM. Alright, Bird.

A Pivot.

(*Out of nowhere,* **SLIM** *sings.*)

SLIM. (*Singing.*)
I CAN'T SLEEP AT NIGHT
'TIL MY BABY COME BACK HOME TO ME
NOO-OO!
I CAN'T SLEEP AT NIGHT
'TIL MY BABY COME BACK HOME TO ME
NOO-/OO!

BIRD. Slim.

SLIM. What? Brother can't sing a little to pass the time?

BLOOD. Hopefully sing better than that.

SLIM. Oh, you don't like my voice?

BLOOD. I like when people sing good.

SLIM. Yeah, well, ain't supposed to be good.

Supposed to be ugly.

BLOOD. Well, that part you got.

BIRD. Ha!

SLIM. You wouldn't know nothing about it no how.

BLOOD. Don't wanna know / neither.

SLIM. *(Cutting **BLOOD** off.)*
I SAID I CAN'T SLEEP AT NIGHT
'TIL MY BABY COME BACK HOME TO ME

(Talking now.) Then Little Walter comes out with the tin sandwich.

(Mimicking a harmonica player.) Phew phew phew, phew phew phew phew / phew.

BIRD. Come on, man.

SLIM. Man, whatever. Y'all not even worthy.

Wasting my talents.

*(To **BLOOD**.)* When you've lived some, then you'll understand some.

BLOOD. I've lived some.

SLIM. Oh, yeah? Tell me what you know then, Blood.

BLOOD. I know whoever sang that song first is the nigga who should stay singing it.

BIRD. Ha!

SLIM. *(To **BLOOD**.)* Where you say your people from?

BLOOD. My people from right here.

SLIM. ...No they not.

BLOOD. Yeah they is.

SLIM. Bullshit.

BLOOD. How you gonna tell me where my people from?

SLIM. You say you don't know who this is I'm singing?

BIRD. He's young.

BLOOD. Ain't young.

BIRD. Well, shid, you ain't old.

SLIM. Nah, he ain't from here is what it is.

BLOOD. Okay.

SLIM. I re-fuse to believe it.

BLOOD. Don't believe it then.

SLIM. Already said I won't.

BLOOD. And, shid, where your people from?

SLIM. Oh, we from all over, nigga.

BIRD. The sticks ain't all over, nigga.

The sticks is the sticks.

BLOOD. *(To* **BIRD.***)* The what?

SLIM. *(To* **BIRD.***)* Best of the best come out the sticks.

Freddie King come out the sticks, didn't he?

BIRD. And was smart enough not to stay, wasn't he?

BLOOD. Who?

SLIM. Greatest bluesman of all time.

BIRD. Let's not get ahead of ourselves.

SLIM. Ain't got to get ahead, behind or beside when you speaking the truth.

BIRD. He was good. Very good –

SLIM. Good?

BIRD. but he was no Muddy.

SLIM. And wasn't trying to be neither!

BIRD. Everyone was tryna be Muddy.

SLIM. Here he goes.

BIRD. No, I ain't going nowhere. All I'm sayin' is –

SLIM. *(Mocking.)* All he sayin' is –

BIRD. wouldn't be no Freddie if Muddy ain't come before him. / That's all I'm sayin'.

SLIM. Oh please! Muddy couldn't do what Freddie was doing.

BIRD. Muddy did what Freddie did and then some while Freddie was still sitting in his mama lap sucking teat. //

BLOOD. Sucking teat?

SLIM. // Okay let me ask you this let me ask you this then. Is it Muddy they call King of the Blues?

BIRD. Nigga what?

SLIM. Is it Muddy Waters they call King of the Blues?

BIRD. Well, that depends.

SLIM. No, no. It's a yes or no.

BIRD. It's not a yes or no. It depends on who the they is that's doin' the calling. That is a vital and critical part of the / argument –

SLIM. Bird, don't worry about the who. / Don't worry about the who –

BIRD. No, I'm askin' "who" because I need to know who it is got in your head that Freddie King was ever considered / to be *THE* King of the Blues. He may be *A* king of the Blues –

SLIM. Time, nigga. The general populace, that's who. Just answer the goddamn question.

BIRD. This is me answering.

SLIM. Is it?

BIRD. And my answer is that that's a mighty big *mighty big* statement you making all by / yourself

SLIM. But it wasn't Muddy, was it?

BIRD. because first of all it's not Muddy or Freddy but ROBERT JOHNSON they call King of the Delta Blues. / And that just goes to show // you – that just goes to show you that you don't know nothin' bout the blues.

SLIM. I'm not talking 'bout – but I'm not talking bout the Delta Blues!

// Show me what? Show me what?

Now I don't know the blues?

BIRD. You don't know nothin' 'bout the blues! I've seen Muddy play! *That* man was a king.

SLIM. You did not.

BIRD. Sure I did. Saw him sing live one time in Baton Rouge. Front row. So close had to wipe his spit off my head.

SLIM. A whole lie.

BIRD. What I got to lie to for?

SLIM. Shid, let you tell it you shared a joint with Chuck Berry and kissed Etta James on the lips too.

BIRD. I did share a joint with Chuck Berry! / But I never kissed Etta. And you never heard me say I did neither.

BLOOD. You shared a joint with Chuck Berry?

SLIM. Oh, y'all on a first name basis?

BIRD. Whatever, Slim.

SLIM. Etta James just calling you up on the phone, huh.

(Mocking.) Hey Bird! Hey Etta!

BIRD. I don't got nothing to prove to you.

SLIM. No, no, no. I know. Etta wasn't the one.

Beverly was your girl.

BLOOD. Who's Beverly?

> (**BIRD** *twitches.*)

SLIM. Who's Beverly? Man, Beverly's / –

BIRD. *(Measured.)* none of your fucking business. Beverly's none of your fucking business.

> (**BIRD** *holds* **SLIM**'s *gaze.*)

SLIM. *(Relenting.)* Okay.

BLOOD. Okay.

> *(Time. Time. Time.)*

SLIM. *(Singing.)*
STONE HEARTED WOMAN,
HOW CAN YOU TREAT ME SO COLD?

> *(Pause.)*

Bird ever tell you why they call him Bird?

BLOOD. You don't stop, huh?

SLIM. Ask him, Blood.

BLOOD. You can't just tell me?

SLIM. Just ask him.

BLOOD. Why they call you Bird, Bird?

> (**BIRD** *doesn't answer.*)

SLIM. *(Re:* **BIRD.***)* Well.

He's just being shy.

> **A Pivot.**

BLOOD. Pretty day.

Hot.

BIRD. Mmhmm.

BLOOD. Nice day for sitting in the shade. Sitting by the water.

(Pause.)

You ever been down there?

BIRD. Down where?

BLOOD. By the water.

BIRD. Nope.

BLOOD. Slim?

SLIM. Nah, ain't never been.

BIRD. All these years living by it, never been in it.

BLOOD. Oh…

I hear it's alright.

(Pause.)

Bet you it be nice and cool on a day like this.

SLIM. Prolly.

BIRD. Prolly.

(Beat.)

BLOOD. You know in Asia they got a black sea? Water dark like midnight. And in Africa, they got a pink river. Can you imagine? Whole river pink. Rose River or something like that, I think. And a red ocean somewhere too. Water look like a jewel. Must be some kind of clean to bathe in red water. Or pink water.

BIRD. Who told you that?

BLOOD. My daddy.

SLIM. ...No such thing.

BLOOD. Yeah, there is. Seen pictures.

SLIM. Young man, I'm telling you. Ain't no such thing.

BLOOD. Well, better be. 'Cause I'm going.

>   (**SLIM** *scoffs.*)

You don't gotta take me serious, nigga. I take me serious.

>   (*Pause.*)

Already got a thousand dollars saved up too.

SLIM. A thousand dollars!

BLOOD. Yup.

SLIM. Where you get a thousand dollars?

BLOOD. I been saving.

SLIM. Sound like you been stealing.

BLOOD. We ain't all the same, Slim.

>   (**SLIM** *sucks his teeth.*)

I'm tryna see some shit, you know?

>   (*Pause.*)

Most people round here, they ain't tryna see nothing but right here. They just wanna know the same people they been knowing, live on the same block they been living and walk the same streets they been walking they whole life. Most exciting thing they got to look forward to is Easter Sunday at church when they get to put on they nice shoes and have everyone say, "Them some nice shoes." And good for them. But that ain't me. No sir. I can't live my whole life waiting on my whole life.

(Pause.)

(A promise.) Just let me get there. Once I get there? Man.

(Pause. **SLIM** *busts out laughing.)*

SLIM. Sound like a nigga who ain't never had no nice shoes.

BIRD. Slim.

SLIM. *(Still laughing.)* Your mama had you in them buster browns front flap always talking, huh.

BLOOD. Don't talk about my mama.

SLIM. *(Still laughing.)* Nigga, I ain't talkin' 'bout your mama, I'm talkin' 'bout them loquacious ass shoes I bet she had y'all in!

*(***BLOOD*** gets quiet.)*

(Still laughing.) And shid, from where I'm standing, look like ain't too much changed for ya since them Easter Sundays, huh? Raggedy as you carry yourself. You need to hurry up and get to that water so you can wash up, nigga!

*(***BLOOD*** is still quiet.)*

(Still laughing.) I mean, am I lyin' or am I dyin'? Bird, look at him. Ol' dusty ass self.

BIRD. You somethin' else, Slim.

SLIM. Oh, please.

(Pause.)

When everyone get so fuckin' sensitive?

A Pivot.

BIRD. Once walked from Oklahoma City to Greenville to see about a somebody.

BLOOD. Greenville in Michigan?

BIRD. Greenville in Mississippi.

BLOOD. Oh yeah?

SLIM. Nigga, you did not walk from no Oklahoma City to Greenville. Shut yo lying ass up.

BIRD. Well, I ain't walk the whole way. I hitched a couple rides here and there. But I would've walked. Would've run.

BLOOD. And when you got there?

BIRD. Told her I made a mistake. Told her I'd rather die than go back without her.

BLOOD. And what she say?

BIRD. Too late.

BLOOD. Damn.

BIRD. 'Nother nigga swooped in. Larry.

BLOOD. Damn.

SLIM. Worst name for a swoopin' nigga too.

BIRD. Mmhmm.

BLOOD. And what'd you do?

BIRD. Got down on my knees. Only time I begged for anything in my life.

BLOOD. But she ain't budge.

BIRD. She ain't budge. Told me to go.

BLOOD. Damn.

BIRD. And I did.

Walked home.

(Pause.)

SLIM. Nigga.

You did not walk.

A Pivot.

SLIM. *(Singing.)*
　　WELL, I AIN'T GOT NO DOLLAR
　　AND I AIN'T GOT NO DIME
　　AIN'T GOT A WOMAN
　　BUT I SURE GOT TIME
　　I BEEN HERE / A WHILE –

BLOOD. Nigga. *Please.*

SLIM. You know you could learn something watching me.

BLOOD. Oh yeah?

SLIM. Voice honey like this? Better believe them bees come buzzing.

It's how I hooked them.

BLOOD. Oh yeah?

SLIM. Oh yeah. This voice?

Man oh man.

BLOOD. Musta been that voice...

SLIM. Mmmhmm.

BLOOD. 'cause it damn sure wasn't them looks!

BIRD. Ha!

SLIM. Nah, nigga, I'm pretty. I'm too pretty.

BIRD. Who's pretty?

SLIM. And, shid, if it ain't the pot calling the kettle black.

BIRD. Ain't no question on that black either.

SLIM. Call me black. I'm the blackest, prettiest motherfucker you ever seen.

BIRD. Well, can't say I've seen blacker. Don't know if they make black blacker than you.

SLIM. And the bitches love me for it.

BIRD. Love you for it? I'm surprised they can see you for it.

SLIM. Man, I ain't worried about what a nigga say no how. I go by what the hunnies say.

BLOOD. Yeah, and what they say?

SLIM. Oh, they love me baby. Hell, can't keep these broads off me with a ten foot pole. Ten foot pole prolly half the problem. If you catch my drift.

BIRD. Nigga, please.

SLIM. Hammerin' Hank way I be batting back these hos. You should see me in action.

BLOOD. I'm / good.

SLIM. Matta fact, what's today?

BIRD. What is today?

SLIM. Come downtown with me Saturday. I'll show you.

BIRD. Is it Saturday?

BLOOD. Man, ain't nobody tryna waste they time watching a old nigga bag a buncha old broads.

SLIM. Oh, Youngblood, I bags the old broads and the young ones too. Slim don't discriminate.

Got enough loving to go round and round again.

BLOOD. Okay, Slim.

SLIM. Round and round again! Tryna tell you.

Might could learn some watching me.

BIRD. Ha!

SLIM. *(To* **BIRD.***)* And I know your old ass ain't laughing.

BIRD. Looking at your ugly ass I sure am.

SLIM. Yeah, yeah, yeah. Just ride with me Saturday. Show you both.

BLOOD. Uh-huh.

SLIM. Bird, your old lady let you out on a Saturday night or do you have to ask her permission? She prolly gotta give you a little allowance or something, huh.

BIRD. What's mine is hers.

SLIM. Oh yeah? What's mine is mine. How about that.

BIRD. I take my vows seriously.

SLIM. Yeah, but do you take yourself seriously, brother?

(Pause.)

BIRD. Do right man get the do right woman.

SLIM. That the kind of woman you got?

BIRD. Don't expect you to understand. We talkin' about what it means to do right by somebody.

BLOOD. Shid, I gotta do right by me 'fore I can do right by anyone else.

SLIM. See, this man got the right idea.

BIRD. But it's a woman make those ideas manifest. When you weary of the world, who gonna hold your head in her lap? Who gonna make sure you fed mind, body and spirit?

BLOOD. I feed myself.

BIRD. Man can't live on bread alone.

SLIM. Man, if you don't get from here with that old geezer talk. Blood don't wanna hear all that.

BIRD. *(To* **BLOOD.***)* You don't want a woman beside you?

BLOOD. I mean I / do –

SLIM. Nigga, I want a woman beside me, underneath me, atop me. Lotta ways I want a woman, if you catch my drift.

BIRD. You don't quit, huh.

SLIM. Listen, Blood, I'm not about that old fashioned shit Bird talkin' neither. Any broad I ever been with, we ain't never have no signed piece of paper between us. Hell, what the law gotta do with what's between a man and woman?

BIRD. Got a lot to do with what's between a man and anything else.

SLIM. I don't need no judge tellin' me what's mine.

BIRD. Judge don't tell you what's yours. Tell you what's not yours. Tell you that land ain't yours, that car ain't yours, that house ain't yours and that broad sitting in that house ain't yours any more than she anybody else's.

SLIM. And that's always been your problem, man.

Put too much faith on the law. Trust the law to tell you what to do, how to be.

BIRD. Maybe if you put more on it, you wouldn't be caught up with it so often.

SLIM. How 'bout I choose to put my faith somewhere else.

BIRD. Yeah, where's that?

*(***SLIM** *thinks.)*

SLIM. Man, in myself, nigga. How about that?

BLOOD. Ha!

SLIM. Oh, I'm somebody, nigga. You can count on that.

Nigga tryna challenge my somebodiness.

BIRD. Man, I don't care *whose* body you is. I'm talkin' about what a man believes in, what he stands on and you gon' say yourself?

SLIM. Myself and these bills in my pocket.

BIRD. *(Incredulous.)* Nigga, what bills?

BLOOD. Ha!

SLIM. Why it's a problem I say what I believe in, huh? I don't come for what you say you believe in. So why is it a problem I say I believe in myself and don't believe in none of that other shit you always talkin' about.

BIRD. It makes me sad deep down in my soul if you really believe there's nothing more to this existence than what you can see and grab with your hands.

SLIM. Nigga, long as I got hands, you better believe I'm grabbing. I'm grabbing everything I can. And yeah that is something to believe in.

BIRD. Man should have a bigger vision of himself than just himself.

SLIM. No, man gotta take care of himself and his own. That's it and that's all.

BIRD. That's what you been doing?

SLIM. Why you so concerned about me and mine all the time, huh?

BLOOD. Come on, y'all. We just talkin'.

BIRD. *(A dig.)* Someone should be concerned.

(**SLIM** *twitches.*)

BIRD. It's a dark and lonely way walking without God.

SLIM. And it's a dark and lonely way walking with him too, nigga.

(Pause.)

SLIM. Shid, I'd know.

> *(Pause.)*

Cell I stayed in didn't have a window. You know what that's like?

> *(Pause.)*

You get one hour outside each day.

First couple of months, it's all you look forward to, you know?

Your sixty minutes in the sun.

But after a while, them months don't begin or end no more.

And after a while, all them hours of sun strung together can't make a dent in all that darkness. You could have God, Allah, Buddha, nigga. Jesus, Mary, all the gods. You could have ten bibles under your cot. Twenty bibles. Don't make more light.

> *(Beat.)*

BLOOD. How long you was away?

> *(Pause.)*

SLIM. Long.

A Pivot.

BLOOD. Pretty day.

BIRD. Hmmm.

BLOOD. What's that?

BIRD. Ain't say nothin'.

BLOOD. Oh.

A Pivot.

BLOOD. Pretty / day.

SLIM. Would you shut the fuck up.

A Pivot.

BLOOD. Pretty day.

BIRD. Mmhmm.

BLOOD. Quiet.

BIRD. The world at peace.

BLOOD. Mmhmm.

BIRD. Just waiting on the next one.

BLOOD. Why you waiting on the next one this one still right in front of you?

BIRD. Laid down my burdens. Settled my debts. I'm just biding my time.

   (Pause.)

I'll have my riches on the other side.

BLOOD. I can't be worried about the other side. Got too much going on this side.

BIRD. Never lost someone, huh.

BLOOD. Not someone so close to me like that, no.

BIRD. Might change your tune.

BLOOD. Natural to lose people. Gotta keep moving.

BIRD. Hmmm.

BLOOD. You lost someone?

BIRD. I lost a lot of someones.

   Too many someones to count.

BLOOD. Well. I'm sorry to hear that.

(**BIRD** *grunts.*)

Slim, you lost someone?

(*No answer.*)

Slim?

SLIM. When I went in, my son was just learning to spell our name. His name is my name, you know. Come out? He a grown ass man. Looks at me like a stranger. Got a kid they say is called Lu. Doesn't even know I exist.

…

Lotta ways to lose someone.

BIRD. Lotta ways.

A Pivot.

(*The sky begins to change.*)

(**BLOOD** *considers.*)

BLOOD. Girl I been knowing say she pregnant. Say it might be mine.

(*Time.*)

(*Time.*)

(*Time.*)

BIRD. Well.

What you gonna do about it?

(*Time.*)

(*Time.*)

(*Time.*)

BLOOD. Send money when I can.

BIRD. That all?

BLOOD. That's all someone did for me.

BIRD. Huh.

> *(Time.)*
>
> *(Time.)*
>
> *(Time.)*

BLOOD. My daddy got out. Left when we was young. Tried to get my mama to go with him but all her family was home – her mama, her sisters, her grandmama and them. And she didn't feel comfortable raising us away, so they split up. And we stayed with Mama, of course. Me and my brothers. But Daddy was after more. He had big dreams, you know. Got to the city. Would call us up and tell us about the apartment we'd stay at on the top of the world 'cause all the apartments was on the top of the world in the city. And he'd tell us about all the different kind of people you'd meet from all over. Nothing like home. Home, everyone from right there where they standing. And all their people from there too, as far back as forever. The only memory they got is of that exact place. That exact porch. That exact road. They ain't never seen nothing like, I don't know, volcanoes and waterfalls. That shit exist right here in the world, you know? Whole mountains exploding with fire and oceans flooding off the side of a hill. And you can stand under one! I don't wanna get to the middle of a bridge and say I lived. I wanna stand underneath a mountain with the ocean falling on my head. Then I *really* lived, you know.

> *(Beat.)*

BIRD. That's gonna be a whole little person come in the world.

BLOOD. I know that.

BIRD. And when they open they eyes, they gonna be expecting to see you.

BLOOD. I'll come around when I can.

BIRD. And if they don't see you where they expecting to see you, that's gonna make them angry.

BLOOD. ...

BIRD. And their anger is gonna consume them and everything they touch. You, too.

BLOOD. I can't do anything about it.

BIRD. You can do everything about it. You can be a man about it.

BLOOD. Lotta ways to be a man.

BIRD. You got it wrong, / Youngblood.

BLOOD. I got four brothers.

Them niggas hungry all the time.

I got a grandma that stay with us and needs all kinds of pills and tinctures and shit.

I got my mama working herself to death just to afford a grave to lay in.

All of that? That's me. I do that. Me.

Lotta ways to be a fuckin' man.

(BIRD is quiet.)

SLIM. It would've been nice if your dad was around, yeah?

(Pause.)

BLOOD. My dad had to go.

SLIM. But it would've been nice if he stayed.

BLOOD. He had to go.

SLIM. But if he took y'all with him. Things would be different.

BLOOD. He had to go.

SLIM. Blood –

BLOOD. I don't even know if the little nigga mine!

BIRD. Make it your business to know.

BLOOD. Nah, I don't feel all that stuff you feel, Bird. All uh that *"bigger is He who is in me."* All uh that? Nah. *I* gotta be the big thing, you know? Ain't nothing bigger here. This is it. I gotta be the big thing. Slim, wasn't you the one said a man got to do for himself and his own? That's all I've ever done. For myself and my own.

SLIM. That is your own.

BLOOD. Nah, I don't believe that.

I don't believe that.

I got things to do, you hear me.

I got things to do.

> *(****BLOOD*** *starts to twitch. His body jerks around. He gags. His legs dance beneath him.)*

SLIM. Hey cool it, Blood.

BIRD. Easy, Blood.

BLOOD. I got things to do. I got –

SLIM. Don't work yourself up, Blood.

BLOOD. I gotta

I got things

I gotta get there

BLOOD. I gotta

SLIM. You gonna get there.

BIRD. You halfway there.

SLIM. Just cool down.

BIRD. Easy, Blood.

SLIM. Just cool down.

> (**BLOOD** *breathes heavily. The others watch him until he settles.*)
>
> *(Time.)*
>
> *(Time.)*
>
> *(Time.)*

SLIM. Wouldn't that be some shit?

BIRD. What?

SLIM. You do all this talking and when you finally get there, wherever it is you think you're heading, ain't nothing there.

BIRD. I won't believe that.

SLIM. Or, better yet, it ain't no different from where you at now. Same dirt road, same grocery.

BIRD. I can't believe that.

SLIM. You get up to them pearly gates, and the big man standing there push them open and it look like just like this look like. Same niggas you always known right there where you left them, cheesing at you, talking about *welcome* and *make yourself at home* and do you have them ten dollars you been owing them all this time?

> *(Pause.)*

Wouldn't that make you...laugh?

> (**SLIM** *laughs.*)

BIRD. Everything's a joke to you, Slim.

> (**SLIM** *sucks his teeth. Pause.*)

SLIM. Ah, it wouldn't be so bad.

> (*The* **THREE** *ponder.*)
>
> **A Pivot.**
>
> (**SLIM** *sings.*)

SLIM. (*Singing.*)
AIN'T GOT A WOMAN
BUT I SURE GOT TIME
I BEEN HERE A WHILE
IF YOU LOOKIN' FOR ME

> (*Beat.*)

Bird ever tell you why they call him Bird?

BLOOD. Nah, he ain't tell me.

SLIM. Bird, tell him why they call you Bird.

(*To* **BLOOD.**) It's a good story.

(*To* **BIRD.**) Tell the story.

(*To* **BIRD.**) C'mon Bird. Just this once.

> (**BIRD** *looks at* **SLIM.**)

Fine, fine, fine.

(*To* **BLOOD.**) It is a good story though.

> (*Beat.*)

BIRD. *(To* **BLOOD.***)* Maybe go see about your someone Monday.

Talk things over.

> *(Pause.)*

BLOOD. Yeah, I can do that.

> *(Pause.)*

> *(Cicadas. The* **THREE MEN** *quietly watch the sunset.)*

SLIM. ...Is it Monday?

BIRD. Think so.

BLOOD. Nah.

Get paid tomorrow.

BIRD. Already?

SLIM. And can't come soon enough.

> *(Pause.)*

Hey Bird, what you doing with your money?

BIRD. Don't ask me what I'm doing with my money.

SLIM. Yeah, whatever.

(To whoever will listen.) Got me a new little piece in New Orleans.

Gonna go see about her.

> *(***BIRD** *grunts. The sun turns in the sky.)*

(To **BLOOD.***)* What about you, Blood?

BLOOD. Huh?

SLIM. What you gonna do with your money?

*(**BLOOD** considers. Takes his time to answer.)*

BLOOD. Gonna buy me a boat.

SLIM. A boat?

BLOOD. Yeah.

*(**SLIM** scoffs. Beat.)*

BIRD. *(About the boat.)* That's gonna be real nice.

BLOOD. I think so.

BIRD. Mmhmm.

(The sun sets on the three men. The light transforming their bodies – blood orange, red, pink, indigo, midnight blue.)

End of Play

www.ingramcontent.com/pod-product-compliance
Lightning Source LLC
Chambersburg PA
CBHW071846290426
44109CB00017B/1945